DOUBLE PORTION

(Power to operate in the next Level)

MICHAEL B. GYEKYE

Double Portion

Copyright © 2015 by Michael Gyekye

Web: www.michaelbgyekye.com

Facebook: my page Michael B. Gyekye

Twitter: @michaelbgyekye

Contact : nanagyekye29@gmail.com

All scriptures were taken from the New King James Bible, except otherwise stated.

Glory Light Publishing, 2015

DEDICATION

This book is a gift of God to all His children, so therefore this book is dedicated to all saints and sons of God who are passionate about God. To God be the Glory.

APPRECIATION

I take this opportunity to express my sincere thanks and honor to my God and savior Jesus Christ, who has blessed me and all of us with spiritual gifts. Also wants to thank my father and Apostle Dr. Emmanuel Owusu, the National Head of the Church of Pentecost and a member of the National Executive Council of the church, and his wife, Mama Patience, who has motivated and inspired me to come out with this book. His humility and love for the ministry has attracted my love and passion for the things of God.

Also to my fathers in the Lord, my District Pastor Osarfo-Akoto of PIWC-NY, my father and my first Pastor in the church of Pentecost Pastor Johnny Ansah, Rev. Dr. Segun Apoeso of Grace Temple Church, Bishop Donkor and Rev. Mrs Donkor of Power House Revival Church, NJ, my parents in the Lord, Mr. and Mrs. Ighedosa, I say may God richly bless you all, also, to my other fathers and mothers in the faith and my web designer and advisor, Tracy Ambrose, God bless you. Also to my dear wife Juliana Achiaa Gyekye and the entire family and children, my friends and all church members, may God richly bless you all.

TABLE OF CONTENTS

FOREWORD

Michael is a man of keen intellectual capability with a staunch and profound fear of God. Come closer and you can deduce the spiritual empowerment so inherited from the power of the Holy Spirit. Having read through the book, it thrills me that he has allowed himself to be used as a source of spiritual empowerment to every young and old Christian for excellent service.

We idolize some people in the Bible and how God used them, as well as some individuals in our generation for the amount of spiritual resources they possess. How we wish we had become like one of them, and how we also think that such people have been blessed by God. It makes us wonder if God loves some people more than others to empower them for His service!

Beloved, the Bible records that God is no respecter of persons and He blesses each and everyone according to the measure of faith. This book will enlighten you as how to get closer to be empowered. You will not receive power if you do not make a move. Michael has attempted in this book to explain how we can get closer to God, the challenges associated with it and the excellent ending when we are home with the Lord.

Precious one, you will be astounded to find the golden thread of receiving power that the Almighty God has woven in His word and the influence it will have over your life in its application, as well as the double portion of power to do extraordinary things. Elijah, Elishah, David, Peter, Stephen, and Paul had it and they did marvelous things. It did not just come after them; they desired it; they longed for it; it is your turn; get a copy of this book, you really need it. I am confident it will motivate and move you forward to better serve the Lord a very befitting way in your generation.

My prayer is that as you read through the pages, may the fire of the Lord descend into your spirit to be on fire for the Lord. And may every hindrance in your life be abased as with a bold heart you approach the throne of God for exploit. Peace and strength of the Lord be yours.

Apostle Dr. Emmanuel A. Owusu
National Head, COPUSA Inc
National Executive Council member, COP

PREFACE

Power is the ability to do any assigned work or job. Any work or assignment, purpose and destiny rely on power. It is the force in operation to execute any job or assignment. This force or power is inevitable in the accomplishment of any mission or purpose in the Lord. In this generation of the later glory, God is seriously moving with much power. There is a supernatural outpouring of the Holy Spirit upon the people of God that both old and young are benefiting, but the choice is in our hands.

> *"And it shall come to pass afterward*
> *That I will pour out My Spirit on all flesh;*
> *Your sons and your daughters shall prophesy,*
> *Your old men shall dream dreams,*
> *Your young men shall see visions. Joel 1:28*

The deception is clear that the devil will fight us tooth and nail to deceive us about these times, but remember we are in the evil days or the last days, but this is the time of the greater outpouring of the gifts of the Holy Ghost. Many faithful ones have been deceived, so many doctrines and teachings are out there, but only the truth can help us to reach our Godly assignment and purpose of God for our lives.

The ancient prophets and men of God operated in power; their words and actions carried so much authority and power that the devil trembled, but now the same cannot be said, sin is having dominion, but may God forbid in Jesus name. Many that provoked heaven, were men and women who knew their times and the conditions that were attached.

Elisha was called by God through Elijah. It was a great calling that left a prosperous farmer Elisha to follow a prophet who had no permanent home even for himself. If your guess is as good as mine, I believe that which was at stake was better than what he had. God can pay what no man can pay.There were many sons of the prophet, but except Elisha.

Deeply meditating on these scriptures *2 Kings 2:2-12*, I got a lot of insights concerning, a call, purpose and the power to operate as a believer in the next level. God gave me many revelations that are found in this book. No matter what the struggles this life brings, with determination and the will of God, we can get to our destination of glory.

As a worker in Christ's vineyard, prayerfully anointed to preach the gospel, I believe this generation needs to hear what God has in stock in this book. This book by the grace of God will put more emphasis on the transference of the double portion anointing from Elijah to Elisha.

INTRODUCTION

For a period of time, I believed that when we say double portion we mean additions of things. If it is a car, you get another one making it double or two cars, as the same may apply to other things; but in some way it is not so. When the bible says double portion, it may also mean second unction or visitation.

For any time there was a second visitation, power was released. Jesus prayed for His disciples the first time, the Holy Spirit filled them, but He told the disciples to wait for the second release. In Acts chapter 2, the second visitation of the Holy Ghost came, this time power was released as it was promised in Acts 1:8. Samson was anointed, but he killed as never before when he got a second release of strength. Double portion is the spirit of persistency and grace to forcibly move mountains that have caused delays, disappointments, frustrations in our lives. Many second visitations released power, so you are next in Jesus name.

Double portion is a state of life, or a state of restoration, where the child of God operates with divine power. Double portion is a multiplication of power to function not an an added factor. When a man receives a double portion, he receives power, and that is to say, multiples of what God has designed for his life.

Elisha said, "Please let a double portion of your spirit be upon me." 2 Kings 2:9

Elisha sought for power not the things of this world. The anointing of Elijah was his target, not the properties of Elijah. What you seek in life, will determine the pace you go. So hopeless people do not make it, they wander. The other sons of the prophet knew Elijah was to be taken out to heaven but they did nothing. Nothing is dangerous. A change is effected if something is done. Do something.

Some analysis suggests that, Elisha did 14 miracles as compared to 7 of Elijah's miracles, but it is more than that. It was all about power to operate at the next level of his life. No one was created a mistake. It took billions of cells to compete in your mother's womb to make you, but you were permitted by God to come here on earth and the same God has not changed or will change. His purpose for you is real, don't give up, but all you need is power, you need the double portion of grace.

Remember the double portion was requested in other to serve a purpose, not for a personal gain or fame, but to make known God's power and ability to save his people not to kill or cheat them.

In this dispensation of grace, God is moving in full force to equip us saints with power to live as according to His will and purpose. Whatever God gives to a man is for a purpose and so it must be guarded with all diligence, fear and total submission to God. Remember we are part of God's plan and so as He said in Jeremiah 1:5;

> *"Before I formed you in the womb I knew you; before you were born, I sanctified you; I ordained you a prophet to the nations."*

This was God speaking to newly called Jeremiah the prophet. He was a young boy and inexperienced, but God called him. God's purpose is to all generations. You are seriously part of your generation. You cannot be left out. You are part of God's plan. You have all it takes to fulfil it; *power!*

Anybody who was called by God operated in His power. Jeremiah taught, he was out of line of purpose, but God created him just for a purpose just as you and I, we are not a mistake or chance but we were created for a purpose. We need His power to operate in His purpose.

Elisha was a farmer, in fact a very rich farmer who had twelve yoke of oxen, in this time of about twelve tractors to his credit as a farmer. He was ok, in terms of living and caring for his needs, he was able to afford all he can get and to also give away, but a purpose driven life led him to meet Elijah the major prophet. Remember, God will not call you when you are idle. Do something, God is counting on you, impossible is not you, yes you can.

We did not come here on earth by mistake, but we were created for a purpose, God created Adam and Eve to multiply and to replenish the earth and to have dominion over God's creation, Noah was also ordained to save himself and his household during the flood, Abraham also was called to be the father of many nations including us believers now and old, Joseph out of his godliness was to save Israel in the time of hunger, Moses was called to save God's people from Egypt , Joshua to break the walls of Jericho, Sampson to deal with the Philistines, David to kill Goliath, Solomon to build the temple etc. and you and I have been called whether small or big to full fill God's purpose for our life. So the key is for us to discover who we are and what God wants to do with our lives.

The power from God is needed in other to be purpose driven. It is not about talk or what you desire to do for man but what

God wants to use you for. Any call of God must be carried out of by His instructions or you fail. Seek the Lord's ways.

In as much as you receive the strength from God, the levels you fly depends on your power levels. Power determines your change levels, your change levels determine your popularity levels. Peter became popular by the power of the Holy Ghost as in Acts chapter 2. He was not fearful anymore. He came out to preach the word of God. Power will outdoor you, it kicks fear away. Until power came upon Jesus, He was still Mary's Son, but as the Holy Ghost anointed Him, God said *"this is my beloved Son."* He went about doing good. You and I need power. Jesus gave us the power to move the gospel from Jerusalem as in Acts 1:8

> **But you shall receive power (dunamis) when the Holy Spirit has come upon you; and you shall be witnesses to Me in Jerusalem, and in all Judea and Samaria, and to the end of the earth.**

What you desire can be given if is in the will of God for your life. Man's power is limited, but God is limitless. You don't have to be discouraged, no matter how long you tarry, it is a better one day in purpose than thousands of days in hopelessness and powerlessness. As you read this book you will be empowered for your next levels, open doors, healing and power will be restored in your life in Jesus precious name.

CHAPTER ONE

The master and the student

To Timothy, a beloved son: Grace, mercy, and peace from God the Father and Christ Jesus our Lord. 2 Timothy 1:2

There is a master and a student philosophy to every man who wants to access power and prosper. There are men and people of God that people looked after to emulate their steps of divine fulfillment. Any greatest man in the Bible, followed a great man.

To become a man or woman of God, in many instances, God places you in the hands of men you have to emulate. There is no one in the Bible who acted alone. Ministry is all about people. Master and student relationship is usually a relationship between a mentor and a protégé, or at least men in strong support and accountability with one another.

It is recorded in many areas in the Bible. In Biblical times, this was the primary way wisdom, skill and Godliness was passed from one generation to the next. This is why the Bible lists many illustrations of mentoring and encouraging relationships between men of purpose. Some mentored their own children as well as some mentored people they adopted as sons in the Lord. Moses is to Joshua, Elijah is to Elisha, Paul is to Timothy, etc.

Masters transfer experiences to their students. No matter how many books we have read, or degrees, experience is the best teacher. It is easy to talk, but hard to do, so experiences speak volume. It will interest you to know that two captains cannot be in one boat; a boat will require one captain. However a captain needs a crew. In any human organization, there must be a master and a student. Without it, we move at a slow pace; lack of support brings loneliness, you cannot go alone. Anybody under you maters, more also those above us, they matter.

Bondservants, be obedient to those who are your masters according to the flesh, with fear and trembling, in sincerity of heart, as to Christ; And you, masters, do the same things to them, giving up threatening, knowing that your own Master also is in heaven, and there is no partiality with Him. Ephesians 6:5,9

A vision that needs fulfillment can never work in isolation. You need people and people need you. The lifeblood of any organization, purpose and vision depend on a dependable master and a subordinate student relationship. The church depends on the youth and the youth depends on the church. I say church because everybody in the church is a potential master. We are all filled with diverse experiences in life.

There are no two masters; there is always a master or a head, blessings move from the greater to the lesser, Hebrews 7:7. Many homes, nations, churches, businesses, corporations and ministries have collapsed now, all because there were many masters and no students or there were many students and no one to teach them.

One way the devil disrupts us believers or the church is to use pride to affect both sides, but may God our Lord forbid that yours will go down the same, but you shall receive power, the double grace of God to survive these times in the mighty name of Jesus.

Elijah and Elisha

And Elisha saw it, and he cried out, "My father, my father, the chariot of Israel and its horsemen!" So he saw him no more. And he took hold of his own clothes and tore them into two pieces. 2 Kings 2:12

Elijah mentored Elisha. They were divinely linked as a father, and a son. Elisha was called by God, but he served under the ministry of Elijah for not less than fifteen years before the

21

mantle fell upon him. Elisha asked to receive a double portion of Elijah's anointing! The request was not for twice the power that had rested on Elijah, but it was a request to operate just as Elijah's replacement, but with much power.

Looking at the intensity and the loss, Elisha was looking for extraordinary anointing; Elisha was looking for a power above powers that will carry him far beyond all forces and oppositions. The request was to be recognized as Elijah's replacement, but the power to serve as an incoming prophet, knowing that his father was going to be with the Lord.

In the days of old, it was common for firstborn children to receive a double portion of their father's estate. This was mandated by the Law, Deuteronomy 21:17

But he shall acknowledge the son of the unloved wife as the firstborn by giving him a double portion of all that he has, for he is the beginning of his strength; the right of the firstborn is his.

Elisha called Elijah *"my father"* in verse 12 of 2 Kings 2. Elisha was asking for the right of the firstborn. Remember, we are all considered His children so we deserve the double portion rights as per the days of old in order to operate in destiny. You are in a rightful position for the double portion, God has no first or second or third son, we are all His sons and children.

Elisha was asking that the same Spirit that had empowered the ministry of this great man of God be given to him as well. Remember, God can use and in most times uses the greater to bless the lesser, Abraham blessed Isaac, Isaac blessed Jacob and Jacob blessed his sons. It is necessary for a father to bless his children or a master to bless his students, this natural flow of blessings will make the latter greater than the former. If children are blessed more than their parents, it is a blessing. No doubt Elisha had double for his master's anointing. Please be humbled and obedient to those above you, leaders of the church and your parents, regardless of their stature, education, positions and titles.

These days I wonder why this flow is altered by pride and covetousness. It is devilish to strife with your father or your master; you will lose big time, the double portion. I don't know where you can go or what you can do, if you have no teacher figure or a father figure in your life. You need experience to overcome experiences. Remember, you wouldn't have been born without a father. The same way any dream must be born through a father figure.

Seeing the Master

What Elisha saw in Elijah, was a factor in receiving the double portion. This is not only what he saw when Elijah was leaving, but the acts of his father Elijah. What you see attracts, draws you closer to learn. Father figure may be controversial by people depending on what they have seen, but what you see boost your commitment levels in order to learn.

Again, wants to say this; your father figure is not a choice by you, you do not choose whom to become your father in the Lord but God chooses you for him to direct you. Eli was a controversial priest at his time, God was even angry at him, yet God allowed Samuel to be directed by him. At the time there was no prophecy, this relationship ended that spiritual famine. Saul was also rejected by God, but David called him father, the anointed. Obey God, not men, you need a father. May our God release one for you now, in Jesus name.

Also, your father or your master may not be another man's father or master, so don't allow what people say disturb you. Elisha said to the sons of the prophet be quiet! My father is different from your father, we are not siblings here. Even among siblings, it depends on how you perceive or see your father.

People will pressure you, they will say all sought of things, but do not allow what people say destroy you and your father, don't even allow what your father has done disturbs you; all you need from him is the needed preparation to replace him. I have come to believe that no matter how anointed you are, or how powerful you are, if your ministry dies with you, you or your student becomes a failure. Look for your replacement.

Elisha died with his ministry, so that was why even his bones raised the dead, all because Gehazi the student became money and pleasure seeker, instead of seeking the double portion. Gehazi became a failure, he saw wrongly, but you shall receive power to operate in your double portion in Jesus precious name! It is necessary my friends and family, for you to get a father figure if you want to fulfill destiny. Our obedience to them is a test of our faithfulness to God and success in life.

Children, obey your parents in the Lord, for this is right. "Honor your father and mother," which is the first commandment with promise: "that it may be well with you and you may live long on the earth. Ephesians 6:1-3

Duty of Master and the Student

The master teaches and the student follows the teachings. The master releases and the student receive. If you do well as a master, you get reliable people to replace you. More also if you do well as a student, you receive double, the knowledge of your master. The teachings of the master are training grounds for greater heights more than the master. Don't run with what you have read, but receive the practicality of it, speak what you have been taught not what you have merely seen, go deeper, be replaceable when you are gone.

Fathers, the same way Elijah found Elisha pursue on a mission to find your successor, son also pursue on a mission to find your father. Isaac called Esau to bless him and to be like him, but Jacob got the blessings; he did not die with it. I remember when I was young in the church; some elders picked up some of us and trained us themselves. The same applied to the young women, now here we are. This relationship is dear to God's heart. This generation must not die. Fathers, transfer to sons, the sons also to their sons, etc. God used them to help us reach where we are now.

When you train up anybody in the ministry, you train yourself; you also create your replacement. As the Lord leads you, your replacement must be better than you.

Remember, we are from glory to glory. The same applies when we loyally obey our teachers or masters, we fulfil destiny. It will be sad to see our fathers dyeing in the Lord with no replacement. We must get another Billy Graham, John and

Charles Wesley, James Mckeown, and the rest in our generation. I drove my pastor's car one day and my prayer was *"Lord, grant me a portion of his anointing in Jesus name"*. All I need is power to operate in my own divine destiny. This power is transferable from one person to another.

Based on the story and sequence of attaining the double portion mandate. That is to say from Elijah to Elisha, this book will seriously emphasize on the story sequence and the places of interest as they moved from *Gilgal* to, *Bethel*, *Jericho* and the double portion at *Jordan*.

CHAPTER TWO

The Gilgal Experience

To every acceleration in life, there is a beginning. This is the starting point. Every journey begins with a step. Sadly, many of us have neglected this step. You cannot wake up, to become a doctor, a nurse or a pilot, but you start from a school. Many visions or dreams depend at this point. Gilgal is the place of beginnings.

2 Kings 2:1-2

And it came to pass, when the Lord was about to take up Elijah into heaven by a whirlwind, that Elijah went with Elisha from Gilgal. 2 Then Elijah said to Elisha, "Stay here, please, for the Lord has sent me on to Bethel." But Elisha said, "As the Lord lives, and as your soul lives, I will not leave you!" So they went down to Bethel.

Elisha began his quest for power at this point. He seriously understood what power was, Jesus said, *we shall receive power,* Jesus left us with power because it is very urgent in our ministry. Elisha knew what he wanted from his master. He saw his master

28

operating in power and so he desired it as the Lord was about to take his father away from him. He knew the God of Elijah and so made up his mind to pursue the journey to obtain the double portion, the *dunamis* which will empower his Godly agenda yet his journey must first start at Gilgal, the place of beginnings, the place you first made the first step.

Gilgal is the place of beginnings; it was here that the Israelites first celebrated Passover in the Promised Land. Here the males born during the wilderness wanderings were circumcised and the covenant was renewed, Joshua 5:8-11

> *So it was, when they had finished circumcising all the people that they stayed in their places in the camp till they were healed. Then the Lord said to Joshua, "This day I have rolled away the reproach of Egypt from you." Therefore the name of the place is called Gilgal to this day. Now the children of Israel camped in Gilgal, and kept the Passover on the fourteenth day of the month at twilight on the plains of Jericho. And they ate of the produce of the land on the day after the Passover, unleavened bread and parched grain, on the very same day*

So looking at the significance of Gilgal, it is the place of beginnings and circumcision. Many people take their beginnings for granted and on the worst note, many dreams and aspirations end at their beginnings because we give up quickly.

This is where decisions and choices are made. This is where the mind is made up on the next step of life. Knowledge at this point is very critical. Your choice is a key, if not frustration and disappointments will affect your life. This is the foundation of your life. If the foundation is destroyed, then the whole structure will be jeopardized. If the foundation is good, then you will have a good structure. Elisha was on target, nothing stopped him, the same way, no one can stop you but you. God's will and purpose are very critical at this level. Open the door of your heart to Him.

Joseph did not become a prime minister in a day; in fact, it took him frustrated experiences and years. The devil will fight you, and he will plant the seed of fear in you to frustrate you at the beginning. But our God is alive; any frustration by the devil is destroyed by the fire of the Holy Ghost.

The beginnings.........

Although beginnings are small, there is an end glory. Most times, things of God may not sound right at the beginning, but will glory at the end. The bible says the glory of the latter house shall be greater than the former as shows in *Hosea 2:9*. Our beginning, although is very important, it will not matter at the latter end glory. Most times, the joy that fills your heart will even make you forget the frustrations and pains which got you there. Just as a woman is about to be a mother, pains will start, but there is joy and laughter in the end. Dear reader, I do not know your beginning, but don't yield to the tactics of frustrations and what people will say, depend on God and make the first step.

Strong Attitude, Self Identity

At Gilgal, discipline, planning and vision are keys of excellence. You cannot go to a place with no invite. You must develop a very strong attitude which will help you pass you on from your Gilgal. At the beginning, you must know yourself who you are and what you want to achieve. Remember Elisha was a student under Elijah. He never for once thought he was greater than his master, but saw something more worthy than pride or disloyalty.

Who you are determines where you are going, where you are going will determine your destination. Take some time to know yourself and develop the student attitude. You must clothe yourself with humility, leave bad company and bad advice from people, they may make you a disloyal student. Remember the sons of the prophet told him to leave his father alone since the Lord was about to take him out, he said be quiet. You cannot be disloyal to your master and prosper in your ministry and even this happen in business and ordinary life.

Many ministries are surviving daily from two to few members instead of flourishing in a double power, anointing of a never ending overflow, all because of disloyalty; that student did not graduate but abandoned the beginning stage of his or her ministry to pursue popularity. Ministry is not a job, but a call. You receive a reward not an award.

These days people are very disloyal, a small church of fifty members will have about ten pastors and each fighting among themselves, every member wants to be a pastor and every pastor wants to be general overseer or the apostle or chairman of the church. God's presence departs from these types of churches. God does not strive with man as in Genesis 6:3

> *And the Lord said, "My Spirit shall not strive with man forever, for he is indeed flesh; yet his days shall be one hundred and twenty years."*

When you enter a church which did not pass through Gilgal you will know, if not you must check yourself. They have no order, there are strives, many divisions over a short time, many rulers and decision bodies, many gossipers and people doing whatever they like in the church. Moreover, there is no vision, no soul winning, no power, no blessings, no testimonies; they are hit so easily by the devil and it becomes home of witches and the worldly class, the house of sin and a den of wickedness. Don't follow these types of churches. You need God at the center of the church and all must submit to His authority.

Remember, the church, your business, marriage, family, etc.; must have its own stage of Gilgal; the place where you began and never forget that. Job 8:7 says *"though your beginning was small, yet your latter end would increase abundantly"*. I personally like small beginnings, I like small churches and big churches and how these ministries begun. Church size does not determine God's size.

Gilgal, a Place of Decision

Your Gilgal is the place of decision. It is obvious that you cannot embark on a journey you have not decided to go, unless you are hopeless, and I think no one is. Ruth made up her mind to follow Naomi, it was against all odds. Naomi was old and she could not produce any more sons, but Ruth made a decision at

Gilgal, and she found Boaz to marry, then they became the great grandparents of Jesus.

But Ruth said: "Entreat me not to leave you, Or to turn back from following after you; For wherever you go, I will go; And wherever you lodge, I will lodge; Your people shall be my people, And your God, my God. Ruth 1:16

Obviously, these days many young ones are affected the most in decision making. Many are laid back due to how they failed in decision making. This has affected their career and destiny. They are singing when they were suppose to be preaching, they are footballers instead of coaching, they are doctors instead of engineers, some are nurses instead of their love to do pharmacy, they are branding people's clothes instead of their own clothing lines.

You are not a mistake here on earth. When you reach or begin at Gilgal, may your love for what you do push you. You should not do what you don't love. You will hurt people. If you love biology, go for medicine or any biology related field, don't allow anybody to push you, not your friends or money. Explain it well to your parents not in disrespect, but with love and respect, they will understand you if you are young and under parental care.

When you begin at Gilgal, know who you are, what you love and can easily do without anybody's influence factors, locate the people you can do for them, do you have any connection? You cannot become a pastor if you are not a Christian, or an engineer if you never solved a mathematical equation before, locate or discover your connection to the thing you love to do.

Apart from connection, invest more of your time to it. Elisha was not discouraged to follow Elijah, you don't have to lose hope, although things may be hard for you, but move on. I always say hard work pays. Until you climb to the top of the mountain, you cannot get a wider view. If you want men to see you, climb higher. Jesus used ships and canoes to preach to people at the beach all because of the view, so He can talk well and more people can see Him.

Invest your time everyday to the things you love and has been called by God to do. I love to see people being blessed, that is why I love to motivate people. I am not happy to see people sad. I do what I do easily, all these am writing, is me and my computer here; I speak freely with compassion to see a change in people's life. My goal is to speak out the change and how you can get there. By the grace of God, I have the wisdom to manage people with no sweat. I deal with all kinds of people, but God is the doer.

God helps me with much wisdom. This book is not for profit, but I want to effect change in your life and my generation. A young man who listened to advice some time ago, gave me a big hug in church all because of the advice I gave him, not to boast but I give all the glory to God. Do what you love with passion.

Someone came to me because he was having problems with his parents because his father was not in support of his marriage. This friend prayed so hard, he did both dry and wet fasting, got all the prophecies right, yet his parents didn't support his marriage.

At the Gilgal of his marriage, he made a choice to go ahead with the support of his uncles went and married this lady. He relied on prophesies and his fastings; am not saying don't fast or follow prophecies; but wisdom is profitable to direct; in other words, direction is a key to a destination.

But I listened to his story, I told him to go back to his Gilgal, the place of beginning to apologize to his parents, this time not to defend himself with any prophecies or from what he has seen in a vision. He should accept the blame and be on his knees to apologize to his parents. Most times we think we know more, but our Bible says *"wisdom is profitable to direct";* you cannot fly without wings. He did that and he texted me to say " *the plan worked".* Check your decision, is it holy and a good way to go?

Follow God and all things shall follow you. Gilgal is a place of decision.

> You will show me the path of life; In Your presence is fullness of joy; At Your right hand are pleasures forevermore. Psalm 16:11. There is a way that seems right to a man, But its end is the way of death. Proverbs 14:12

Circumcision and Uncircumcision

Gilgal is also known as the place of circumcision and I want to go further from here.. Circumcision signifies holiness or cleanliness as the Spirit of God enables me to understand; uncircumcision also means uncleanliness or unholy. Circumcision and uncircumcision has both old and new testament significance in the bible. The special meaning of circumcision for the people of Israel is found in Genesis 17 and occurs within the context of God's renewed covenant promise to Abraham, following the initial contractual relationship (Gen. 15). On the second occasion, God again promised lands and offspring to the still childless patriarch, and gave him the sign of circumcision, which was to be imposed upon Abraham and his descendants as a token of covenant membership as in Gen 17:10.

This is My covenant which you shall keep, between Me and you and your descendants after you: Every male child among you shall be circumcised;

Circumcision qualifies you to be part of the Abrahamic blessings. Circumcision opens the door for the blessings, whereas uncircumcision closes the door of double portion. In this dispensation, although is neither circumcision nor uncircumcision, that avails anything, but its significance of holiness and righteousness still either opens the door for our blessings or closes the door to our blessings. The double portion grace is to the circumcised children of God. Those who have given their lives to Christ, who has invited Jesus Christ into their hearts; these are the citizens of the double portion grace. You cannot start a journey in the Lord without the circumcision of your heart, it must be all for God.

Circumcision was a religious rite and was intended to mark the beginning of covenant solidarity for Abraham's descendants rather than describing the historical origins of the procedure. When Greek paganism threatened to swamp Judaism some two centuries before Christ was born, circumcision became a distinctive indication of Jewish fidelity to the covenant. Thus John the Baptist was circumcised in Luke 1:59, as were both Jesus in Luke 2:21 and Saul of Tarsus in Philippians 3:5 on the eighth day of life, making them accredited members of the covenant people.

Circumcision permits God to function on your behalf; it enables revelation and knowledge to fall upon your head. That is the reason why people who has the call of God must be spiritually circumcised so that they may be separated from the unclean thing.

To be circumcised is to leave the world alone to fulfill the heaven's call, to leave sin alone to join into God's righteousness. You cannot sin and be proud of obtaining the double portion, sin has the capacity to destroy you into death if not taken care of; Gehazi's double portion was lost due to sin, he failed at Gilgal, sin took over his destiny and so leprosy took over, but you shall not fail your generation at Gilgal but will be separated from sin for God's double portion over your life.

The Sin Problem

Why do we need to be circumcised? It allows us to be purged from sin. Circumcision has to do with the removal of the flesh, but cutting it out of the body. Sin is the flesh that has to be dealt with. Remember from creation that God created man both male and female God created them as in Genesis 5:2

He created them male and female, and blessed them and called them Mankind in the day they were created.

God created man both male and female; when man disobeyed God, he was demoted from the glorious nature of God and then flesh came to dwell with man. Remember man became uncomfortable with the new member *flesh*, so he felt he was naked. God loves man, but hates *flesh* that is to say the desire to sin. Remember what I am explaining here is a mystery that needs the power of the Holy Ghost to understand. Let us look at Genesis 6:3, 12

And the Lord said, "My Spirit shall not strive with man forever, for he is indeed flesh; yet his days shall be one hundred and twenty years." So God looked upon the earth, and indeed it was corrupt; for all flesh had corrupted their way on the earth.

Before then man was referred to be like God for He said *"Let's make make in our own image"* Genesis 1:26-28. But in this verse man is referred to as *flesh*. The problem of sin is the loss of God's presence. Indeed, God's redemption of man, is to destroy flesh that has become part of man, from Genesis 7:21

And all flesh died that moved on the earth: birds and cattle and beasts and every creeping thing that creeps on the earth, and every man.

Flesh is the sin of disobedience that puts a man into nakedness, shame, curse and destruction. When anyone yields to the flesh, he or sins against God; the flesh will tell you to fornicate, steal, hate, etc. for everyone is doing it, but you will die as a result, if you do them. Mr. Flesh has an agenda on its own; looking at Galatians 5:19-21

Now the works of the flesh are evident, which are: adultery, fornication, uncleanness, lewdness, idolatry, sorcery, hatred, contentions, jealousies, outbursts of wrath, selfish ambitions, dissensions, heresies, envy, murders, drunkenness, revelries, and the like; of which I tell you beforehand, just as I also told you in time past, that those who practice such things will not inherit the kingdom of God.

Romans 6:23 says the wages of sin is death; that is why God sent His Son Jesus to die in the flesh, so we can operate as the glorious men of God's initial creation. Jesus is a complete God who could have come in the Spirit or in any other form, but He came to destroy flesh so we can be redeemed back to God.

The flesh was crucified, it was bruised and tortured for our spirit's man's sake, it was split into, pierced and was brought to open shame so on the third day, we will rise in a newness of life, to take back our glorious position just as what God originally created us. So if you are in Christ, you are not under the flesh of sin anymore, but a child of the most high our God Almighty. To move in double power, your flesh must die. Let us look at it carefully in this scripture; I believe you will understand it very well;

Ephesians 2:1-9. *And you He made alive, who were dead in trespasses and sins, in which you once walked according to the course of this world, according to the prince of the power of the air, the spirit who now works in the sons of disobedience, among whom also we all once conducted ourselves in the lusts of our flesh, fulfilling the desires of the flesh and of the mind, and were by nature children of wrath, just as the others. But God, who is rich in mercy, because of His great love with which He loved us, even when we were dead in trespasses, made us alive together with Christ (by grace you have been saved), and raised us up together, and made us sit together in the heavenly places in Christ Jesus, that in the ages to come He might show the exceeding riches of His grace in His kindness toward us in Christ Jesus. For by grace you have been saved through faith, and that not of yourselves; it is the gift of God, not of works, lest anyone should boast.*

If you understand this scripture, then you will notice here that if you are a believer, then you have been spiritually circumcised into the commonwealth of the saints in Christ by grace; then you are no longer under sin but rightfully sit together with Christ in the heavenly places. Don't allow the love of sin deny you of your double portion of God's favor over your life.

Character and the Anointing

We cannot ignore the character of Elisha which led him to the double portion of Elijah's anointing. He had perseverance and knew what he wanted. When we look at 2 Kings 2:4-5, we can identify how focus and serious he was,

Then Elijah said to him, *"Elisha, stay here, please, for the Lord has sent me on to Jericho."* But he said, no way Papa! *"As the Lord lives, and as your soul lives, I will not leave you!"* I have waited for this opportunity for a long time. So they came to

Jericho. Now the sons of the prophets who were at Jericho came to Elisha and said to him, *"Do you know that the Lord will take away your master from over you today?"* So he answered, *"Yes, I know; keep silent!"* that is to say "If you guys don't see, as for me I see". Perseverance is the key, aside humility and passion.

For us to get the double portion, we must possess a good character. Our character must be intact, while others were talking Elisha was seriously following his master, he did not allow the pressure of the sons of the prophets to interfere with his quest to obtain such a divine inheritance. In these days, we can easily lose focus. Things around us, news, TV shows, gossips, friends, mobile phones and their apps can easily discourage us, but dear one, be of good cheer, make up your mind and the Spirit of God is there to help you.

In the ministry, many young workers in the Lord are very disloyal. Many young pastors I have come across and have worked with have strange and unguided characters. They carry very strange characters; they behave badly, but when they think they can prophesy and perform miracles, they are ok. A pastor friend told me he invited a pastor to his program and when this pastor came to stay in his house he wanted to sleep with his sister. This same pastor or prophet went ahead to propose to all the ladies who came to sing in the program. But this prophet is still able to go around prophesying so he thinks he is ok. It is a lie from hell; remember the devil is a deceiver. We are accountable to God as stewards in His vineyard.

We are just vessels, in this case container of God's power, we will be judged not by the anointing, but by our character here on earth so we must be careful. We must depart from evil; Proverbs 14:16

A wise man fears and departs from evil, But a fool rages and is self-confident.

Sampson was very anointed, but failed in character, so he perished with the Philistines, the same way Saul was anointed by the Prophet Samuel, but character failed him, Gehazi was meant to get double of Elisha's but he failed. Your success is linked to your character. You don't have to be in a hurry to become somebody, live the life you want to become. It is better when you are recommended than you recommending yourself. So live well among men, so the double portion of God's next level in ministry can come to pass your time in Jesus name. Look at what Paul said about his son in the faith, the junior pastor Timothy;

Philippians 2:19-22, *But I trust in the Lord Jesus to send Timothy to you shortly, that I also may be encouraged when*

I know your state. For I have no one like-minded, who will sincerely care for your state; for all seek their own, not the things which are in Christ Jesus, But you know his proven character, that as a son with his father he served with me in the gospel.

Character and anointing cannot be separated, you may preach well, dance and praise well, recite all scriptures, play all the instruments in the church, if you have a very bad character, time will tell, but you cannot go far. You will be denied you next levels. It is not witches, but you. Bishop Oyedepo of Winners Chapel, Nigeria said; *"capacity can take you there, but character can keep you"*. Remember, at your Gilgal, you are a beginner; you either choose to go forward or you fail to attain double power.

Under mentorship you automatically adopt or operate in another man's power so you can operate in double power. You must be loyal in other to receive the full benefits. Deal with any disloyalty in you when under mentorship. Elisha was loyal to Elijah to the point that there was no separation. Gehazi separated from Elisha and he received leprosy.

You do not have to end in Gilgal, you are about to go to Bethel, circumcised yourself, depart from evil, watch what you decide to do, be of a good character, be morally right before God and man and your next level will not be denied.

CHAPTER THREE

The Bethel Experience

According to A. W. Tozer, We need a baptism of clear seeing. We desperately need seers who can see through the mist of Christian leaders with prophetic vision. Where there is no vision, there is no hope as according to George Washington Carver. Helen Keller says, *"The most pathetic person in the world is someone who has sight, but has no vision"*. This is what we call spiritual blindness. Vision is the fuel for success. You seriously become what you see. That is to say, when you see right. Change comes when you are able to see the change you desire. Jacob saw the Lord at Bethel.

> *Then Elijah said to Elisha, "Stay here, please, for the Lord has sent me on to Bethel." But Elisha said, "As the Lord lives, and as your soul lives, I will not leave you!" So they went down to Bethel.* 2 Kings 2:2

Bethel is the place of vision or dreams; the place where you meet or see God. It is a place of divine encounter. It is a state of one's life, where he or she experiences a divine encounter. It was here that Jacob met God and dreamed and saw angels descending and ascending out of heaven, Genesis 28:18-22;

Then Jacob rose early in the morning, and took the stone that he had put at his head, set it up as a pillar, and poured oil on top of it. And he called the name of that place Bethel; but the name of that city had been Luz previously. Then Jacob made a vow, saying, "If God will be with me, and keep me in this way that I am going, and give me bread to eat and clothing to put on, so that I come back to my father's house in peace, then the Lord shall be my God. And this stone which I have set as a pillar, shall be God's house, and of all that You give me I will surely give a tenth to you."

To possess power, you need an encounter. Power is given by one with higher authority. Jacob met God and after that divine encounter, Jacob established a covenant with God; he was full of energy to pursue his next level. Any divine encounter empowers us. The apostles on the day of Pentecost, power came and they flew in the power of the anointing. They were hiding, but received boldness to stand in open places to preach the word.

But you shall receive power when the Holy Spirit has come upon you; and you shall be witnesses to Me in Jerusalem, and in all Judea and Samaria, and to the end of the earth. Acts 1:8

The power we have as believers in its real terms is greater than the word *power* in general terms. We have been given authority which is above the usual *power* we know. An area champion who operates in that area is ok until when the Governor of that area who is a man of authority comes, he becomes just a mere man even though he has power. We as Christians are ambassadors of God on earth. We govern not as mere men. Man was created with power and dominion over things of creation, to multiply and be fruitful. We as believers have authority to operate in destiny or our God given purpose.

Seest thou a man diligent in his business? He shall stand before kings; he shall not stand before mean men. Proverbs 22:29

Elisha saw many miracles in the hand of Elijah so he knew what he wanted. Most of us became stronger in the faith based on several encounters we had; miracles and some mind bordering testimonies we had or heard of. What energizes us on

50

the course to receive the double portion is the divine encounter. That is to say, events you encounter that beats the physical mind, a mind bordering experience. In this case Elisha saw chariots of fire, his father was just carried away through the skies. This is a mind bordering isn't it?

One of my sisters in the Lord felt an inner power, some kind of electric power in her, and all of the sudden she found herself in front of the church to give her life to Christ, after that her life had a turn around, and I believe strongly that you are next to receive the next miracle in Jesus name.

The Assignment

Our awesome God is a planner and His purpose for you began since your formation in your mother's womb. No matter how you came on earth, whether you came from a single mother, a prostitute or out of wedlock, you are not a mistake; our God has perfectly designed a purpose for you. Our purpose is our assignment on earth; what the Master requires.

> *"Before I formed you in the womb I knew you; before you were born, I sanctified, you; I ordained you a prophet to the nations."* Jeremiah 1:5

51

There is a call on every Christian life; the Bible says *"many are called"*. This is a call to be a Christ like in various jurisdictions. We are one body but many parts; some are the eyes, nose, ears, mouth, tongue, but the same head, some are hands, stomach, legs and feet, but we are all one body to serve our master Jesus Christ in faith love and strength.

We have the same call, but different assignments. Every assignment has instructions attached. When a man received a call from God, there are instructions that must be followed in order to receive the grace to multiply in such assignment. God told Jeremiah that before He formed him, his assignment was already known to Him. But in Jeremiah 1: 17-19 some instructions were given;

> *"Therefore, prepare yourself and arise, and speak to them all that I command you. Do not be dismayed before their faces, lest I dismay you before them. For behold, I have made you this day a fortified city, and an iron pillar, and bronze walls against the whole land-- Against the kings of Judah, against its princes, against its priests, And against the people of the land. They will fight against you, but they shall not prevail against you. For I am with you," says the Lord, "to deliver you."*

God's instructions enable us to prevail. When the mantle fell on Joshua God gave him instructions, in Joshua 1: 1-2, 8, the bible says

> *After the death of Moses the servant of the Lord, it came to pass that the Lord spoke to Joshua the son of Nun, Moses' assistant, saying: "Moses My servant is dead. Now therefore, arise, go over this Jordan, you and all this people, to the land which I am giving to them--the children of Israel. This Book of the Law shall not depart from your mouth, but you shall meditate in it day and night, that you may observe to do according to all that is written in it. For then you will make your way prosperous, and then you will have good success.*

An instruction attached to a call makes it a success if obeyed, not the call itself, remember many has been called. If we follow the instruction we prosper. God told Moses to point the rod, but when anger took over, he failed to operate in the instruction, and he never saw the Promised Land. It will surprise you that many hear the call, but forbid the strings attached. There is always a work after a prophecy. Most times we yearned for the sweet aspect of it, neglecting the bitter aspect, if only we are prepared to follow the instructions, our bitterness will be turned into sweetness in Jesus name.

I once met a pastor who told me in a group of Christian students that he fasts every day; that is the instruction God gave him. Joshua was to obey, observe and to meditate upon the word of God day and night, so that his duty or call will be a success and prosperous.

Watching the Genuine Call

Let each one remain in the same calling in which he was called. 1 Corinthians 7:20

There are three things one must know about any divine assignment. The call of God is *personal*. Anytime God calls or develop a burning desire upon anyone, he calls personally. Abraham was called personally, he alone was called. Let us look at Genesis 12:1-4

Now the Lord had said to Abram: "Get out of your country, from your family and from your father's house, to a land that I will show you; I will make you a great nation; I will bless you and make your name great; and you shall be a blessing; I will bless those who bless you, and I will curse him who curses you; and in you all the families of the earth shall be blessed."

Also, we can also look at Isaiah 51:2

"Look to Abraham your father, And to Sarah who bore you; for I called him alone, and blessed him and increased him."

Also, there are *instructions* attached. These instructions define the assignment. Noah had such instructions, not to forget about Abraham, Moses, Joshua, Sampson and Jesus gave the disciples instructions and the order by which the Holy Ghost will come upon the disciples. Let us look at a prophet who forbade God's instructions in 1 Kings 13. This prophet of the Lord was supposed not to eat, but the king said to the man of God, "Come home with me and refresh yourself, and I will give you a reward." But the man of God said to the king, "If you were to give me half your house, I would not go in with you; nor would I eat bread nor drink water in this place. For so it was commanded me by the word of the Lord, saying, *'You shall not eat bread, nor drink water, nor return by the same way you came.'*

But another prophet who was dried of God's word forced him to disobey, and lions met him on the way to devour him. Many ministries have been devoured, local or global ministries. They now lack the oil of success because they are out of order, no mission, they are self centered. On the third note, although a call is *personal* and there are *instructions* attached; a call from God is *peaceable*. James 3:17

> **"But the wisdom that is from above is first pure, then peaceable, gentle, willing to yield, full of mercy and good fruits, without partiality and without hypocrisy".**

Any call is the wisdom of God for man. A call after empowerment or ordination needs wisdom. Book knowledge and expertise have limits. That is to say, the ministry is not your burden, but God's burden so you need His steps not yours. My church is a living proof. Any ministry surviving on man's strength is not from God. It is God who calls not man. This is the reason why Moses got into trouble, he thought he was the one in charge so he acted on his own anger and God forbade him not go to the promise land although he prayed and fasted many times, God has to bury him Himself. Whether consciously or unconsciously we must allow God's will to perfect our call.

Measure every church or personal ministry by the trouble free management, if they have to suffer to even pay rent, buy church products, lack of resources, force members to give, they cut off their light, and one problem after the other; all these and others are signs of churches and ministries out of order, they may have the call but they have their own steps.

I am not saying your ministry will not suffer trials and tribulations, but, even in your trials and test times as a ministry if God is in it, the storms will not overflow you, it is not our ministry or church but God. Jesus will surely arise for your sake in Jesus name. We must allow God to take over, not us, we will die, but the church will still be there, even if we foundered the church, we will go so hand it over to God.

Godliness, the Gateway

For bodily exercise profits a little, but godliness is profitable for all things, having promise of the life that now is and of that which is to come. 1 Timothy 4:8

Godliness is the gateway that opens the door for your double portion. As a servant or a child of God, Godliness cannot be negotiated. It serves as the foundation for the supernatural and

57

the operations of signs and wonders. It is not magic, but for your prayers to be answered, Godliness is the key. I have seen people who pray, but Godliness differentiates those with good report and those who doesn't.

One day God told me, have you seen a child fasting to get something from the father? The answer is no; fasting regularly is good, but godliness is a key to perfect fasting. I had a father, though he is gone to be with the Lord; there was not once I have to fast to receive something from him. I don't have to fast to eat, or for money for my upkeep. I just ask, seek and knock, but if we forfeit our rights as sons of the Most High God due to ungodliness, we suffer.

All I know about my father is that, he has anything I can ask. I don't have to check his bank account before I ask for money. He gives to me because of my rights as his child. The same with God; if you lose your rights in the Lord, you lose answers to prayers.

> *Beloved, now we are children of God; and it has not yet been revealed what we shall be, but we know that when He is revealed, we shall be like Him, for we shall see Him as He is. And everyone who has this hope in Him purifies himself, just as He is pure* 1 John 3:2-3

Godliness is non-negotiable when you want to experience the double portion of God's favor in your life. Your purification enables your next levels. Don't be deceived with this evil doctrine of once saved forever saved and so grace has covered it all. It is true, we are living under the dispensation of grace, but remember, he that is in sin, is of the devil. 1 John 3:8 says *"He who sins is of the devil, for the devil has sinned from the beginning.* The grace of God repositions us into the righteousness of God in Christ.

Godliness with contentment is great gain, as a man or a woman of God, flee from carnality and worldly things to pursue righteousness, Godliness, faith, love, patience, gentleness. God's divine power has been given to us all; things that pertain to life and godliness, through the knowledge of Him who called us by glory and virtue. May your Godliness open the door of your double portion in Jesus name!

Godliness is a mystery hidden at this end time or generation. In 1Timothy 3:16, the Apostle Paul told Timothy *"without controversy great is the mystery of godliness"*. Godliness is the key to unlock the windows of heaven to rain down blessings on an individual committed in the things of God. You can be higher in spirit in your own eyes, pray and fast for days, weeks, months and years, but if it goes without Godliness then is a time wasting. We did not know before, but I think now we know.

Titus 1:1 Paul, a bondservant of God and an apostle of Jesus Christ, according to the faith of God's elect and the acknowledgment of the truth which accords with Godliness,

1 Timothy 6:3 If anyone teaches otherwise and does not consent to wholesome words, even the words of our Lord Jesus Christ, and to the doctrine which accords with Godliness,

Remember, whoever or whatever you do in the Lord, your attitude must be accorded with Godliness.

Connecting with the Greater

> ***Yet it is beyond all contradiction that it is the lesser person who is blessed by the greater one.*** (Hebrews 7:7 AMP)

I encountered this scripture some years ago and it has become a great source of discovery for me. It says your blessings or your double portion is in the hands of a greater or a better one. Then the next thing is to discover who is the better or a greater one. It is simply the one who has or can lead you to what you want (a rich man if you want to be rich, the mother with children if you want to have children, the pastor or any servant of God, if you want or desire to be one etc.) is the one who has it. Elisha could have left longtime, but he remained with Elijah. Your extraordinary is found in the ordinary, the supernatural is in the natural. It takes a natural man to be supernatural. There are no limits for you in Jesus name.

God is our ultimate source and so He is our greatest provider, but He works using men to help you. Your next level has been deposited in someone or in a man of God. God has positioned them for you, and until you discover them, you are deprived of your double portion; but may our God forbid in Jesus name!

Connecting with the father's in the Lord

Remember Bible makes mention of two parents in Ephesians 6:1-3.

> *Children, obey your parents in the Lord [as His representatives], for this is just and right. Honor (esteem and value as precious) your father and your mother— this is the first commandment with a promise; that all may be well with you and that you may live long on the earth.*

61

There is a parent in the Lord and parents, those who gave birth naturally to you. I like connecting with men whom the Lord has given to me as fathers in the Lord. These are men whose life and commitment in the things of God are good to follow. Some are my mentors, but others I follow their lifestyle and teachings. They greatly minister to me a lot. Remember, Elijah was a father to Elisha and Apostle Paul to Timothy; in both cases it was the father and the son relationship.

And Elisha saw it, and he cried out, "My father, my father, the chariot of Israel and its horsemen!" So he saw him no more. 2 Kings 2:12

Elisha obtained the double portion and Timothy was able to manage such powerful church as a young man in the Lord. Our generation is in trouble and very confused, because we are teaching the old as biblically, it is not suppose to be so. Most of us do not have the teachable spirit. It was not so with Elisha, you have to still remain under the school of divine double favor if you want to experience it. You must first be a student before you can become a master. Remember Jesus grew in knowledge, you must also grow, it is not magic, and you must climb the steps of the double unction one by one. Each step has something new to learn. Many younger brethren are under the bondage of delay, frustration, pain, sorrow and the major forms of obstacles because they have not connected to their fathers in the Lord. Pray, God will show you someone whom you can learn from.

Connecting with your pastor

And I will give you pastors according to mine heart, which shall feed you with knowledge and understanding. Jeremiah 3:15

Pastors are not made, but they are given by God to feed us with the needed knowledge and understanding that will take us to the Promised Land. Pastors are like Moses, who was the mediator between God and the Israelites. They teach, care, guide, intercede for us; moreover, they also pray and fast for the church. In the hands of these parents, God can enable your double portion, how do you treat your pastor? Repent and draw unto God and He will lift you up.

I was shocked to hear that someone sent a text message to insult the Apostle of the church. This is a curse. Remember, even though God was not pleased with Eli, He still used him to confirm His blessings to Hannah's barrenness, Prophet Samuel's mother obeyed and he was blessed. Elisha had one Pastor Elijah, by following and focusing on his directions, the double portion came. Only God is to be worshipped, but He uses His men. I mean men of God. Connect with your pastor, my dear, you will not loose.

I love my pastors no matter how controversial they are, that is their human side, but I am after the spirit, because, I am in the spirit. Some pastors may allow the flesh to dictate to them, but, so long as they operate as pastors over your head, give them the needed respect. You are not a judge, they belong to God. Forbid people who preach against, gossip and those who insult their pastors and church leaders.

Please don't join those groups, they are very dangerous. There is only one Pastor in heaven and the devil who was a member, he rebelled and fell. If you want your double portion of grace to the level fall out of your hands, then follow these people; but my prayer for you is that, you will not follow any person, group or any association who speaks against the pastor.

CHAPTER 4

The Jericho Experience

Then Elijah said to him, "Elisha, stay here, please, for the Lord has sent me on to Jericho." But he said, "As the Lord lives, and as your soul lives, I will not leave you!" So they came to Jericho. 2 Kings 2:4

Jericho is a place of conquerors. When you reach here, every wall, no matter how thick must respond to God. With determination Elisha purposed in his heart to go further into his double portion of Elijah's anointing. There were many sons of the prophet, but they became observers instead of achievers. My God shall give you courage for you to reach your Jericho in Jesus name.

Jericho was the place near Jordan, where the Israel had its first military victory in the conquest of Canaan as in Joshua 6. Jericho was also a border town. To pass beyond this location was to enter a wild zone new territory. Moreover, it is also a place of past victories; a place of conquering.

Jericho is a border or barrier between success and failure, promotion and demotion, winning and losing; Joshua needed to conquer in order to get to the Promised Land. Don't worry, in life when you face a Jericho wall, they come in other for us to depend on God more than ourselves.

Somebody's Jericho may be poverty, sickness, demotion, hunger, obstacles, temptations, trials of different forms, persecution and demonic obstacles, but no matter how they come; we are more than conquerors through the strength of our Lord Jesus Christ.

God had a strange plan for the battle of Jericho. He told Joshua to have the armed men march around the city once each day, for six days. The priests were to carry the ark, blowing trumpets, but the soldiers were to keep silent. On the seventh day, the assembly marched around the walls of Jericho seven times. Joshua told them that by God's order, every living thing in the city must be destroyed, except Rehab and her family.

All articles of silver, gold, bronze and iron were to go into the Lord's treasury. At Joshua's command, the men gave a great shout, and Jericho's walls fell down flat! Joshua 6:1-5. The Israelite army rushed in and conquered the city. Only Rehab and her family were spared.

I don't know the battle you are in right now at this point of your double portion; you shall conquer in Jesus name! But you will conquer without the arm of man's effort. David killed Goliath, but there was no sword in his hand. 1 Samuel 17:50;

remember also the battle is the Lord's not yours, 2 Chronicles 20:15. Our trials promote us to the next level; they are mountains when we climb, we get into higher realms. Trials are not punishment, but grounds that will lead us to the next level of double glory. James 1:12 says;

> *"Blessed is the man who endures temptation; for when he has been approved, he will receive the crown of life which the Lord has promised to those who love Him."*

This verse says blessings attach every trial or temptations; we don't get them when we give up, but when we endure and if we have been approved, we receive the crown of life. Also, it says if we love God we need to endure trials, out of it our God refines us as gold. Trials and temptations are part of Christianity. You shall overcome them as says in Psalm 34:19

Dealing with Jericho walls

According to one of the men I love so much, Ben Carson, in his book, Gifted Hands: The Ben Carson Story, he said; *"Success is determined not by whether or not you face obstacles, but by your reaction to them. And if you look at these obstacles as a containing fence, they become your excuse for failure. If you look at them as a hurdle, each one strengthens you for the next."*

He later stressed that; *"Successful people don't have fewer problems. They have determined that nothing will stop them from going forward."* He became acutely aware of his unusual ability, his divine gift, his belief, his extraordinary eye and hand coordination. He said "It is my belief that God gives us all gifts, special abilities that we have the privilege of developing to help us serve Him and humanity. And the gift of eye and hand coordination has been an invaluable asset in surgery". "I'm a good neurosurgeon. That's not a boast but a way of acknowledging the innate ability God has given to me. Beginning with determination and using my gifted hands, I went on for training and sharpening of my skills. "

Jericho wall is the representation of your last hurdle into destiny, purpose and vision, is either you conquer or fail to reach your dream. You have come far to fail here. You have tried many times, but you cannot give up at your Jericho.

How you confront that situation is very important. When I was in school one of my Jericho walls was money. It became an obstacle to reaching my goal to become what I wanted to be but I was able to graduate with a first class.

Money answered to all things, but the love of money can destroy your dream. We must be careful, money can lead us astray, but lack of it also can delay your dream, may God open the windows of heaven for your sake in Jesus name.

How can we deal with our Jericho walls? Let us look at these;

By Prayer and Fasting

And he said unto them, this kind can come forth by nothing, but by prayer and fasting. Mark 9:29

Some things come forth as a result of prayer and fasting. On the other hand, this same verse tells us some things, you don't need to fast or pray for them. Why? You don't need to fast before you run from an impending sin like adultery, stealing, lies, etc. you have to run away just as Joseph did, but in this case we are focussing on fasting. We fast to receive and to allow some things to come forth. Let's look at one of the greatest men of prayer in the bible, Daniel.

> *In the first year of his reign I, Daniel, understood by the books the number of the years specified by the word of the Lord through Jeremiah the prophet, that He would accomplish seventy years in the desolations of Jerusalem. Then I set my face toward the Lord God to*

make request by prayer and supplications, with fasting, sackcloth, and ashes. Daniel 9:2-3

I once said that *"man is very careless"*. Most times we wait till problem comes before we fast and pray, not so with Daniel, he was a habitual faster, from the time he entered Babylon, he began to fast and pray, no wonder he had many promotions.

One of the most effective ways in dealing with our Jericho wall is by engaging in persistent prayer and fasting life. You never know when the devil may strike, but your prayer bank will answer for you. Daniel was confronted with the bondage of slavery of his people, with consistent prayer and fasting life, seventy plus years of slavery came to an end.

"Is this not the fast that I have chosen: To loose the bonds of wickedness, to undo the heavy burdens, to let the oppressed go free, and that you break every yoke? Isaiah 58:6

Elijah was a man with a nature like ours, and he prayed earnestly that it would not rain; and it did not rain on the land for three years and six months. James 5:17

Elijah was a man of prayer, he prayed earnestly for no rain, but has also prayed again for abundant rain. Your prayer can either shut the mouth of your enemies or opens it when you don't pray.

When we pray, we engage in a dialogue with God, where we hear His mind and we follow His word. You cannot command God to do what He does not want to do, you command just as according to His will. Many prayers have gone wrong all because we spoke and we never yielded to God's will, but prayer must go as according to God's will.

> *Now this is the confidence that we have in Him, that if we ask anything according to His will, He hears us; and if we know that He hears us, whatever we ask, we know that we have the petitions that we have asked of Him* 1 John 5:14-15

Most times when we pray, we do not know what we are praying about. Somebody may pray for money, but at that point is not money that he needs, but wisdom to operate on what he already has. If the Widow of Zarephath knew that the oil in her house could make her rich, she wouldn't have prayed to enjoy her last meal and die.

Also, we may pray for a child, but we should pray for God to make us an effective mother or father to children we come across. If you have no patience, you cannot be an effective parent, also if you cannot appreciate God as the provider of children, is also likely you cannot have one.

A child or children are not a justification to prove a better or good marriage, remember your parenting figure can draw men both young and old to you. But you will be wasting time praying for a child without the ability to become a parent. These days, people pray for husband and wife, without checking their character. Instead, pray "Lord, create in me a clean heart". Character is what attracts a wife and a husband to you. In this season of double portion, you shall get answers to your prayers in Jesus name! But remember to allow the Holy Spirit to lead you to pray also pray in the Word.

And he said unto them, this kind can come forth by nothing, but by prayer and fasting. Mark 9:29

True fasting brings down self, but it elevates your spirit. It breaks the power of the flesh and demonic yokes; but builds you up in the spirit. Remember your flesh has power; it is called the will power, your ability to make choices that concerns life.

72

Fasting that accompanies prayer and the word of God is a great tool for your spiritual growth. It sensitizes your spirit man.

Fasting and prayer kills unbelief and speedily bring answers when nothing else is working. Esther was an example; what fasting and prayer can do. Esther and the Jewish people fasted for three days, and as a result Haman's plot fell upon him. Ezra the priest fasted for God's protection while carrying valuable things for God's temple. We too can fast for God's protection (Ezra 8:21-23);

Daniel the prophet fasted for the fulfillment of God's promises, and received mighty revelations from God. (Daniel 10:3); Elijah needed to fast 40 days before he heard God's voice again (1Kings 19:8). Moses fasted 40 days and nights in order to receive the Ten Commandments and the Laws of God, and to see God's glory and goodness. Jesus fasted fasted forty days and nights before embarking on His mission. (Matthew 4:1-10; Luke 4:1-13).Jesus says to us in Matthew 6:16, "When you fast..." not "If you fast". A true disciple of the Lord will fast at regular times, this will make us spiritually sensitive. For your double portion, prayer and fasting is non-negotiable.

By Praises and Gratefulness

Remember with praises the Jericho walls came down. How do you feel when people praise you and also when they express their gratitude to something you have done for them? I believe you will be sincere and answer like I will. You will feel awesome and wants to help or provide more even if you do not have it; all because of their gratefulness. When we praise God, it pushes Him to open the windows of heaven for more rain. In life, we become limited when we are not grateful for what people do for us, no matter how small or big.

The story Jesus told about the servants and talents, it can also be related to gratefulness, the ungrateful becomes weak to the extent that, that which is in his hands becomes unproductive.

Ungratefulness can cost you; your double portion; Just as Gehazi. Elisha was grateful to his master, he followed him to Jericho. It is good to thank people and express your gratefulness when they give you gifts, although we should not demand it, but it is necessary, it opens the gate for more gifts. Our God is holy and He deserves all the praise.

But you are holy, Enthroned in the praises of Israel.
Psalm 22:3

The above scripture tells us that wherever there is praise to God, He comes to occupy his seat there. In the praises, He shows up. What happens when God shows up for? For Jacob His destiny was changed, for Manoah Sampson was born, for Moses, the era of captivity came to an end. No matter what, when God shows up, all becomes, well, your double portion gets accomplished, signs and wonders prevail, your enemies are put down.

I will call upon the Lord, who is worthy to be praised; so shall I be saved from my enemies. Psalm 18:3

The opposite works; without gratefulness and appreciation, God's presence vanishes. Energetic, heavenly focused praise and worship enforces the presence of the King with the host of angels to minister to us. Sometimes when you enter into some churches, these are the signs; a praise-less church is a very ungrateful church. Miracles happen in a praise church, they always have a testimony.

Most times I worship and praise God with my own songs and words of praise. Sometimes I change the words of some songs for my own. I love praise and worship; I learn how to play the bass guitar myself by the grace of God, all to praise our maker. God shows up to help you when you praise.

By The blood and the Word of our Testimony

"And they overcame him by the blood of the Lamb and by the word of their testimony, and they did not love their lives to the death" Revelation 12:11

The blood and the word of our testimony are also weapons in dealing with our Jericho walls. Our testimony expresses our gratefulness to God and the expression of His power among men. So testimony time is expedient anytime we meet in church, we should allow it in church every Sunday not some days. From the above verse we realize the effectiveness of testimony and the Blood of the Lamb.

He took the Testimony and put it into the ark, inserted the poles through the rings of the ark, and put the mercy seat on top of the ark. And he brought the ark into the tabernacle, hung up the veil of the covering, and partitioned off the ark of the Testimony, as the Lord had commanded Moses. Exodus 40:20-21

In Exodus, there was the ark of the Testimony behind a veil, in the tent of meeting; these were placed in the ark. This was written on tablets and God instructed Moses to place them in the ark of covenant and remember the ark of the covenant, became the symbol of the presence of God. So where testimonies are shared, the presence of God becomes available and so He operates as to the benefits of the covenant.

We must also know that the Blood is our weapon in dealing with our Jericho walls. The blood of the lamb was applied in Goshen, and the angel of death passed over the people of Israel in Egypt.

Now the blood shall be a sign for you on the houses where you are. And when I see the blood, I will pass over you; and the plague shall not be on you to destroy you when I strike the land of Egypt. Exodus 12:13

What it means here is that, the opposing force to death at that time was the blood. In this end time covenant, the blood of our dear Lord Jesus is our weapon. I see that many false prophets can use the name "Jesus" but cannot toy with the Blood of Jesus. Jesus is the Mediator of the new covenant, and to the blood of sprinkling that speaks better things than that of Abel. Hebrews 12:24

Anytime we pronounce the blood, we invoke the authority of the Blood that speaks more than the blood of Abel to work on our behalf. This Blood purchased us, cleansed us, sanctified us, and gave us boldness to enter the Holiest of Hollies and to give us life everlasting. The devil flees when you speak the blood. The Blood is our defense in this wicked world. The thief comes to kill, steal and to destroy, but the Blood of Jesus gives life, for there is life in the Blood.

By Engaging the Armor of God

In dealing with life's eventualities, we may face many Jericho walls; these are life struggles if not taken care of, will create a massive wall of obstruction which will oppose the effectiveness of God's provisions over our life. Let us look at Paul's letter to the Ephesians.

> *Finally, my brethren, be strong in the Lord and in the power of His might. Put on the whole armor of God, that you may be able to stand against the wiles of the devil; "For we do not wrestle against flesh and blood, but against principalities, against powers, against the rulers of the darkness of this age, against spiritual hosts of wickedness in the heavenly places".*
>
> *Therefore take up the whole armor of God, that you may be able to withstand in the evil day, and having done all, to stand. Stand therefore, having girded your waist with*

truth, having put on the breastplate of righteousness, and having shod your feet with the preparation of the gospel of peace; above all, taking the shield of faith with which you will be able to quench all the fiery darts of the wicked one.

And take the helmet of salvation, and the sword of the Spirit, which is the word of God; praying always with all prayer and supplication in the Spirit, being watchful to this end with all perseverance and supplication for all the saints — and for me... (Ephesians 6:10-18, 19-20 NKJV)

In this letter to the Ephesians, our Apostle is using an analogy to compare a Christian's spiritual weapons, the armor of God, to the standard armor and sword of a Roman soldier. Every soldier is trained, specialized enough to win battles, no matter the size, shape and nature of their opponents. You must know who you are, your strengths and weakness, and to also know your opponent and the type of war at hand. Some fight world wars, others spiritual wars, some are also peacekeepers, and the type of war determine the type of ammunitions you must use.

Apostle Paul clearly stated who our enemy is, the type of war and the ammunitions we need; the whole armor of God, not some. First, we must stand, and to stand is to get ready or set you for battle; it is not sleeping matter.

Moreover, you must be truthful; this is spiritual identity, Jesus we know, Paul we know but who are you? Then you must be right with the Chief commander, without righteousness, you are out of order. You cannot sin and win battles against the master tactician of sin, Satan.

You must be pure in dealing with your Jericho walls. Also the peace from God must reign in your heart. If you belong to the army of God, be still and know that our chief commander neither sleeps nor slumber and so we have nothing to worry about. Where there no peace, there is no strength, where the presence of God is, there is liberty, peace and joy.

And what shall I more say? For the time would fail me to tell of Gideon, and of Barak, and of Samson, and of Jephthae; of David also, and Samuel, and of the prophets: Who through faith subdued kingdoms, worked righteousness, obtained promises, stopped the mouths of lions. Quenched the violence of fire, escaped the edge of the sword, out of weakness were made strong, waxed valiant in fight, turned to flight the armies of the aliens.
Hebrews 11:32-34

Faith as a shield is very essential, the former soldiers of God who through faith subdued kingdoms, worked righteousness, obtained promises, stopped the mouths of lions. Quenched the violence of fire, escaped the edge of the sword, out of weakness were made strong, waxed valiant in fight, turned to flight the armies of the aliens; they did it all through faith.

Faith is practiced when we are trusting and obeying God to the fullest; believing the impossible to be possible; by Him all things were made. By faith the walls of Jericho fell down, after they were compassed about seven days. Hebrews 11:30

Every time they passed through a city, Elijah even attempted to get Elisha to stay, but his faith became a force for him to move on. The distance between your dream and fulfillment is faith. Faith is the substance of things hoped for, the evidence of things not seen. For by faith the elders of old, including Elisha obtained a good report. Although Elisha's faith helped him this wasn't an effort on Elijah's part to hinder Elisha's progress, it was designed to test his faith. These were opportunities for Elisha to stop and to settle down, but he did not, the double portion was his goal. I pray you never miss God's time in your life.

You need to be decorated by the helmet of salvation. The world awaits for the manifestations of the sons of God and he that is born of God overcomes the world and this is the victory that overcomes the world, even our faith; your position as a child of God qualifies you as an overcommer as in 1 John 5:4. It surprises me those who operates in the church, with no clear identity in Christ, it is very dangerous.

We don't have to be silent when we are asked to declare our identity as children of God. Salvation is the key to total liberation. Smith Withglesworth once said in his book as I paraphrase, anytime the devil tells you are not a child of God, it might as well be it is a confirmation that, you are a child of God. You need to be born again in order to assess the benefits of the kingdom of God.

The sword of the Spirit is the word of God. It is a weapon which can never be negotiated for anything. The Spirit took Jesus in the wilderness, and the devil came to tempt Him, but He overcame by the Word. To pray you need the word, to give and to receive, you need the word, to dance, walk, operate in this life you need the word of God and from God to empower you.

God said, and all came to pass; it is but by the power of His word. Simon said, "but by thy word" and he caught fishes he has never caught in his entire life. The Spirit of God is behind His word, that is why He can send His word and signs and wonders follow. We must key in His word in dealing with our Jericho walls.

We must pray always, not sometimes or when in the middle of troubles; we must pray without ceasing. You must be prayer full person in order to overcome your Jericho walls. No amount of prayer is wasted, continue, your victory is on the way. We must be watchful as we pray, we must persevere in prayers, and intercede for the saints; our other fellow believers.

"Our critics make us strong! Our fears make us bold! Our haters make us wise! Our foes make us active! Our obstacles make us passionate! Our losses make us wealthy! Our disappointments make us appointed! Our unseen treasures give us a known peace! Whatever is designed against us will work for us!"

— Israelmore Ayivor, The Great Hand Book of Quotes

CHAPTER 5

The Jordan Experience

Jordan is the place of death. Somebody may say, I don't want to die, but this is not the death we know of, but it is a place of settlement. A place where you need not to run anymore. You settle here. Here is where you receive your double portion.

It is a place where goals have been realized; a place of supernatural accomplishment. The Jordan river represented the boundary of the Promised Land. To cross it meant to enter into death. Whether you like it or not, everyone of us will enter this place. Either we receive the crown of glory or the eternal punishment. You will always be settled on something.

It was a formidable barrier that few would ever want to cross. Elisha did not see his master anymore at Jordan. At this point, you will not remember your struggles anymore, you enter into rest, hopes and aspirations are accomplished. You walk in divine power and authority. At this point you bear the marks of victory.

Then Elijah said to him, "Stay here, please, for the Lord has sent me on to the Jordan." But he said, "As the Lord lives, and as your soul lives, I will not leave you!" So the two of them went on and fifty men of the sons of the prophets went and stood facing them at a distance, while the two of them stood by the Jordan. Now Elijah took his mantle, rolled it up, and struck the water; and it was divided this way and that, so that the two of them crossed over on dry ground.

And so it was, when they had crossed over, that Elijah said to Elisha, "Ask! What may I do for you, before I am taken away from you?"

Elisha said, "Please let a double portion of your spirit be upon me." So he said, "You have asked a hard thing. Nevertheless, if you see me when I am taken from you, it shall be so for you; but if not, it shall not be so."

Then it happened, as they continued on and talked, that suddenly a chariot of fire appeared with horses of fire, and separated the two of them; and Elijah went up by a whirlwind into heaven. And Elisha saw it, and he cried out, "My father, my father, the chariot of Israel and its horsemen!" So he saw him no more. And he took hold of his own clothes and tore them into two pieces. 2 Kings 2:6-12

Elisha didn't ask anything at Gilgal, Bethel and Jericho, but in Jordan. This makes here, the place of double portion. He has to cross Jordan the to reach the zone of settlement. Most times we find ourselves in these same places in our walk with the Lord. Trials and troubles tend to turn us away from the love of God, but they are valleys and mountains helping to get us to our place of double portion. In Christ, we suffer to survive, but Satan will make you to survive for a while to suffer for long. I will choose to suffer and spend eternal life later.

Far too many believers spend their entire Christian lives at Gilgal. They never grow and they never leave the place of beginnings. They always look at past accomplishments. Some even go as far as Bethel but they catch the vision of God's great work which must be done. At this point they receive all kinds of prophecies, but fail to work on them. They see the need, they feel the tug, but they never get past the place of dreaming about what they might do.

We have many of our younger brothers and even older die only reaching Bethel. They never take the next step of making those dreams and visions into realities. Still others hold onto their Jericho's. They live in the victories of yesterday. They remember what happened back there, forgetting that, the same God who blessed them is desiring to bless them again. There is always room for further achievements and accomplishments. You don't have to give up. You need to get to Jordan. Christ is still the same yesterday, today and forever.

Then some come to Jordan. This is the barrier between the self-life and the Spirit-life. Few ever take that final step of faith and sell out to go with God all the way. Notice that of all the prophets, only Elisha had enough faith to cross the river and go with Elijah, and it was Elisha who received the double portion. Don't allow the opportunities to settle down along the way to hinder your progress, but by faith, proceed with God and watch Him remove the barriers. I pray we all get to our Jordan our place of settlement in Jesus name.

The Glory of the latter rain

> *"For thus says the Lord of hosts: 'Once more (it is a little while) I will shake heaven and earth, the sea and the dry land; and I will shake all nations, and they shall come to the Desire of All Nations,[b] and I will fill this temple with glory,' says the Lord of hosts. 'The silver is mine, and the gold is mine,' says the Lord of hosts. 'The glory of this latter temple shall be greater than the former,' says the Lord of hosts. 'And in this place I will give peace,' says the Lord of hosts."* Haggai 2:6-9

The Lord says once more, meaning once again, it is your double portion of grace to occupy the glory of the latter rain. The Lord will shake heaven for your sake. The windows of heaven will open for your sake. Remember, God is never late, from experience, I believe he reserves the best for the last. They had a wedding and on the third day Jesus showed up, he turned water into wine and the people complained, why they have reserved the best for the last. That is what God can do, He reserves the best for the last, He will never give you the best in the beginning, any level you are now, remember there is a next level even the clouds and the skies have levels, so I pray for your next levels.

In the list of the elders of Hall of Faith; Abel, Enoch, Noah, Abraham, Isaac, Jacob, Sara, Joseph, Moses, Rahab, Gideon, Barak, Samson, Jephthae, David, Samuel and the prophets, all these people had their beginning, they suffered, they were rebuked just as Elisha was, they were beaten and insulted, also their family was on the line, their reputation got low to the extent some lost their figure or personality, but by faith, they got to their zone of settlement.

But may the God of all grace, who called us to His eternal glory by Christ Jesus, after you have suffered a while, perfect, establish, strengthen, and settle you. 1 Peter 5:10

The Lord settled these men of faith. They entered their Jordan. They hoped for the eternal glory. By faith, they got there, some here on earth others waited for the eternal glory.

Abraham was called to a country he didn't know the boundaries, wealth or the opportunities there, he suffered from the beginning many ups and downs, this *call* nearly destroyed his marriage and family but he hoped for the latter glory to become the father of many nations. We have to endure the prize to enter into glory.

By faith Abraham obeyed when he was called to go out to the place which he would receive as an inheritance. And he went out, not knowing where he was going. By faith he dwelt in the land of promise as in a foreign country, dwelling in tents with Isaac and Jacob, the heirs with him of the same promise; *for he waited for the city which has foundations, whose builder and maker is God* Hebrews 11:8-10.

Vision, Purpose and Achievement

Vision is the act or power of anticipating that which will or may come to be. Purpose can be related as the reason for which something exists or is done, made, used, etc. It is the determination; resoluteness about the use of a particular object. When a vision or purpose is accomplished, then *achievement* is completed. Elisha was eying his master only to see the anointing of God falling upon him; nothing could distract him, not even the son of the prophets or Elijah.

Whiles some of us run away from our purpose, some who have discovered who they are, what they can do, whom they can do for, and where they are going, have achieved many results. The use of our life is not self-satisfaction, but how we can affect the lives of others.

In fact, it takes a lot of work for God to prepare one man for Himself. God has to prepare Moses, who was a murderer and quick tempered, made David a king at the expense of his love for women, Jacob who was a liar. Mysteriously, God was preparing them for an effective assignment. The same way God is preparing me and you to face our purpose here on earth. Remember we were not created by an accident, but for a reasonable purpose after which we go back to God.

> *"Now when David had served God's purpose in his own generation, he fell asleep; he was buried with his ancestors and his body decayed"* Acts 13:36 (NIV)

God's purpose for you is His plan for you and so it applies to each and every one. Elisha was prospering as a farmer, but God had a different agenda for him.

> *For I know the plans I have for you," declares the LORD, "plans to prosper you and not to harm you, plans to give you hope and a future.* Jeremiah 29:11 (NIV)

God's plan is to give us hope and a future, a plan to prosper us and not to harm us. If we fall into His plan, we prosper in everything we do, we operate in total rest; but if we do not, then we die, every aspect of our life dies.

> *There is a way which seems right unto a man, but the end thereof is the ways of death* Proverbs 14:12, 16:25

This scripture is reflected twice in the same book, meaning it needs our attention. God gave us the will to make choices. If these choices made out of God's will, will bring a great damnation, but if we will agree with David in Psalm 16:11
You will show me the path of life; In Your presence is fullness of joy; At Your right hand are pleasures forevermore.
Our vision is what we have seen concerning the future. Our vision defines our purpose, and then when we develop into our purpose, it turns into an achievement. There is no doubt that Elisha knew what he wanted from His master Elijah. So when he was asked, it did not take him more time to ask what he wanted. It is sad when some of us stand to pray and fast, but we do not

know what we want. We need to discover what we were made to achieve in this life.

Vision sees into the future concerning what God wants our life to be. Commit all your ways not some to God.
Jesus knew what He came here on earth to do. In Luke 4:18-19 He declared the words of His own prophecy in Isaiah 61:1, 2

> *"The Spirit of the Lord is upon Me; because He has anointed Me; To preach the gospel to the poor; He has sent Me to heal the brokenhearted; To proclaim liberty to the captives; And recovery of sight to the blind, To set at liberty those who are oppressed; To proclaim the acceptable year of the Lord.*

Jesus came on a mission. A mission to rescue us from the oppression of poverty, broken hearted, captivity and blindness; so if you are in Christ, then you are entitled to overcome all these oppressions; my prayer for you is to overcome all these in Jesus name.

Jesus knew what to do. What do we know concerning our life? No wonder He told the mother on the third day of the wedding in Cana of Galilee, *"Woman, what does your concern have to do with Me? My hour has not yet come."* John 2:4.

Jesus mission or purpose on earth was also timed, many times He refused pressure from family and people by telling them His time is not yet up. Wait on God to discover yours, your discovery will lead to your recovery, and your recovery will enable your prosperity.

Road to Discovery

Moses knew he was a deliverer, that was why he has to kill to deliver, but that was not in God's will for him. God's timing was different. His plan led to death, but when God's time came, He was made a god to Pharaoh. So the Lord said to Moses:

See, I have made you as a god to Pharaoh, and Aaron your brother shall be your prophet. Exodus 7:1

This was Moses walking into destiny a life of purpose. On the road to discovery, you must commit to the will of God concerning your life. If there is anything to start, start with prayer. Pray into your future and purpose.

Secondly, seek the word of God concerning your passions, spiritual gifts, dissatisfactions or burdens in this life as you engage with people and as you pursue this life. God has a plan for everyone. Your plan is not too far from what you are

93

naturally passionate about, it is not too far from the gifts you spiritually have from God through prayer and fasting.

There are certain things that dissatisfy you naturally. Moses has to kill, because he did not want his brother to be under bondage of suffering and persecution. Some people are helping the church growth now because certain things dissatisfy them. Some are pastors, prophets, evangelists, etc. all because of this discovery. I have seen medical doctors, pharmacist, architects, industrialists, bankers, nurses, teachers, who have put all their knowledge and prestige down to pick up the cross across the globe.

Dissatisfaction can lead to discovery. The sons of the prophets were standing aside, Elisha went ahead for the double portion all because of the dissatisfaction of standing by to see this great anointing pass by, others knew it, they prophesied it to him but, he pursued for it. You don't have to be a spectator and expect to score a goal. You have to be on the pitch. You cannot sit home and expect the church to grow, you have to act. Your purpose is your action, they are your passions. The things you are passionate about.

When you talk to some musicians, they will tell you, I started singing when they were young. Sometimes they will tell you *I love music*. Why? They are pursuing what they are passionate about. You cannot be what you are not passionate about. Elisha was overjoyed, left a very prosperous farming into the ministry of prophecy with passion.

> ***So he departed from there, and found Elisha the son of Shaphat, who was plowing with twelve yoke of oxen before him, and he was with the twelfth. Then Elijah passed by him and threw his mantle on him. And he left the oxen and ran after Elijah, and said, "Please let me kiss my father and my mother, and then I will follow you." And he said to him, "Go back again, for what I have done to you?" So Elisha turned back from him, and took a yoke of oxen and slaughtered them and boiled their flesh, using the oxen's equipment, and gave it to the people, and they ate. Then he arose and followed Elijah, and became his servant.*** 1 Kings 19:19-21

Our passion maintains joy and happiness, without passion, you may see a common thing a burden. The disciples were very passionate about their call; they were beaten but still they were happy to move on. Passion is a force, it energizes and refocuses you. You don't have to see singing in the choir as a burden; you don't have to be a *burden* pastor or an apostle. Get rid of your burden with passion. May God release strength now into your passions in Jesus name!

But the manifestation of the Spirit is given to each one for the profit of all: I Corinthians 12:7.

Your spiritual gift speaks into your discovery. They tell you about what the master requires from you. God gave them to you to profit you; remember God's plan is not to harm you, but to prosper and give you hope; so your spiritual gifts must not be operated with carelessness, it is what the master wants from us. You don't have to abuse the power.

But we have this treasure in earthen vessels that the excellence of the power may be of God and not of us. 2 Corinthians 4:7

Our purpose is a treasure hidden that needs discovery. I pray that as you pursue this discovery with prayer and fasting, God will hear and will show you as in Jeremiah 33:3

'Call to Me, and I will answer you, and show you great and mighty things, which you do not know.'

Our God has promised to show us when we call to Him. Call unto Him and He will show you in Jesus name.

Working on the double portion

It is one thing to discover but there another thing to work on the anointing. To work means to labor, to serve and not to be a lord in the anointing. I always say, the higher you go from a member in the church to become a deacon, elder, pastor or an apostle, the greater responsibility you take, you become a servant into the members; some ignorant leaders want to lord over their members. We are servants of God, but service to the members. We will be rewarded by our works not positions or titles.

> *Therefore, my beloved brethren, be steadfast, immovable, always abounding in the work of the Lord, knowing that your labor is not in vain in the Lord.* I Corinthians 15:58

Initial Oppositions

It will be sad if you cannot pursue in the God given purpose. You know it, you have it, but the stumbling blocks are so huge that you cannot go ahead. One of my fathers in the Lord told me *"Mike, when God gives you a mandate, you will face so many oppositions"*. At that time I had two hot oppositions that only the grace of God can see me through. God did it, I overcame. Apostle Paul had the same; let us look at I Corinthians 16:5-9

97

After I go through Macedonia, I will come to you—for I will be going through Macedonia. Perhaps I will stay with you for a while, or even spend the winter, so that you can help me on my journey, wherever I go. For I do not want to see you now and make only a passing visit; I hope to spend some time with you, if the Lord permits. But I will stay on at Ephesus until Pentecost, because a great door for effective work has opened to me, and there are many who oppose me (NIV).

Apostle Paul's mission faced many oppositions; inside the church and outside the church. Some people think all will be well, bread and butter. That is what we pray for, but God prepares you on many grounds. He will allow you to pass through the waters and the fire. Your dignity and ego will be tried, but after it all, you will be refined for the master's use.

When I got saved, I faced inside and outside oppositions in the church; some of my friends left but some also stayed. I was in the church one day and an Elder came and insulted me, he told me to get out the sanctuary, it is not a place for kids. Wow! I was a new convert but I looked to Jesus. This man saw me climbing higher in the Lord. He later has to acknowledge me.

Any problem confronting you now will bow to you in Jesus name!

> **And Elisha saw it, and he cried out, "My father, my father, the chariot of Israel and its horsemen!" So he saw him no more. And he took hold of his own clothes and tore them into two pieces. He also took up the mantle of Elijah that had fallen from him, and went back and stood by the bank of the Jordan. Then he took the mantle of Elijah that had fallen from him, and struck the water, and said, "Where is the Lord God of Elijah?" And when he also had struck the water, it was divided this way and that; and Elisha crossed over.** 2 Kings 2:12-14

After receiving the double portion, he faced the waters. He has to cross over the Jordan to operate in the double portion. Then he took the mantle of Elijah that had fallen from him, and struck the water, and said, *"Where is the Lord God of Elijah?"* And when he also had struck the water, it was divided this way and that; and Elisha crossed over.

> **But may the God of all grace, who called us to His eternal glory by Christ Jesus, after you have suffered a**

while, perfect, establish, strengthen, and settle you. 1 Peter 5:10

Anytime you face any obstacle, speak the Word of God. Jesus overcame by the Word, so we have the authority to operate with the word. In one of my encounter, I came to Isaiah 43:26, *"……..declare thou and that may be justified".* I stood upon this word and changed a whole letter of termination into a promotional letter.

Everything answers to the Word of God; the wind, the waters, storms, fire, trials, troubles, temptations, sickness, poverty, etc. What you declare is backed by the power behind the Word of God.

Double Portion is for you to grab

Double portion is not a number or an addition but a walk in dominion in every aspect of life. It cannot be measured by numbers, but by how much power you have at hand to affect your purpose and generation. Samson was just a man, but his strength was doubled to defeat the Philistines. Also, David was anointed just as Saul, but he killed Goliath instead of Saul. In fact, Saul as qualified and anointed to defeat Goliath, but the strength of David was doubled to kill Goliath.

Double portion is yours to grab, Elijah did not tell Elisha to follow him to receive the double portion but he desired for it. As you desire, the Lord will help you to receive the grace to operate in the double portion. *Shalom!*

The grace to access your double can only come from God, by you surrendering your life to Jesus Christ. You can surrender your life by confessing your sins and accepting Jesus Christ as your Lord and Saviour. That way, you will be born again and the grace to access your double portion will effectively be made available to you. If you want to be born again, say this prayer and mean it from your heart:

"Dear Lord Jesus Christ, I come to You today. I am a sinner. Forgive me of my sins and cleanse me with Your Blood. Deliver me from sin and Satan to serve the living God. I accept You as my Lord and Saviour. Make me a child of God today. Thank You for accepting me into Your Kingdom."

If you prayed this simple prayer, you are now a child of God. You have gained access to receive your double portion. God loves you and will never leave you. Read your Bible daily, obey

God's Word and seek Christian fellowship (John 14:21), a church for that matter to attend.

Congratulations! You are now born again! All-round rest and peace are guaranteed to you, in Jesus' name. Call or write, and share your testimonies with me through my email or call me at 3479205004 / nanagyekye29@gmail.com.

Watch out !

Upcoming Books;

1. Let there be Light

2. Afflicted but Lifted

3. Power in the Blood

Made in the USA
Middletown, DE
28 July 2015